Shawneesha Cooper

Grabbing Bondage by The Throat

Unless otherwise indicated, scripture quotations are paraphrased from the King James Version of the bible as derived from https://biblegateway.com

Definition references are paraphrased versions derived from https://lexico.com and https://dictionary.com

Grabbing Bondage by the Throat

Imprinted: Independently Published
Printed in the United States of America
ISBN: 979-8-218-43136-5
For booking visit: www.outpourglobal.com

Walking out our Freedom

Dedication

I give all praise to God. Thank you, Lord, for trusting me with the gift of teaching and providing many avenues of expression to enhance others. I thank you for teaching me and giving me the courage to write unashamedly. I am so grateful to be your daughter and a tool that you are using to be glorified.

Love your daughter.

To my mom:
I never got to share this with you, but God used you too, I was able to become the best version of myself from our life experiences together. I hope when I come to heaven we can talk about it.

Love your only Daughter.

Table of Contents

Introduction

This book contains real-life stories of trauma and complete testimonies that have taken years to build up the courage to face and confess. The journey of life can be very difficult to navigate, but somehow, we manage to conquer the things that come to conquer us. I encourage you to take this journey with me and face your past fears while gaining tools to be triumphant in your life. In this book, you will discover tactics and weapons to use against your adversaries and enemies. We have the power and are no longer victims.

Grabbing Bondage by The Throat

Walking out our Freedom

Chapter 1
Facing Abuse Head-on.

_Y_ou never understand how life is going to turn out, especially when you are going through tough times. My life has taken me on a journey, with some ups & downs but a lot of downs along the way. I have seen so much in such a brief time; I did not know how I could find my way out of the hole I was in, but fate knocked on my door.

My life growing up was not the kind of life I would have wanted to experience; I should say live but to me, everything was an experience there were few moments to live. I was stuck in a place where I could not see my way out, but I was constantly hoping for a way to escape. Why is it that when a person is abused, the first question they ask themselves is, what did I do to be treated like this? The truth is you have not done anything but that is always the first question you ask yourself.

Sometimes because of all the things you are facing you think of yourself as weak & hopeless, but you are really the opposite of that. I looked over all the things that I have been through, and I can proudly say that God was there for me every time I needed Him. He stopped me from dying to everything that had me bound. He stopped the enemy from possessing my soul and destroying my life. In my hardest times, I could not see God but after He brought me out, I looked over everything that happened in my life, and then I could see Him as clear as day.

How do you love someone who is knocking down your confidence, putting you down, and cutting you deep with sorrow? The only answer I have is only through the grace & mercy of God. God's love keeps you from building up hate in your heart. When you have lived in an abusive life, it can cause a person to look for other ways to escape the atmosphere around them. Drowning themselves in drinking, drugging, and abusing their bodies. Only to escape what is in front of them for a little while, this is called a temporary fix and it will not change the past you are so desperately trying to escape.

I have understood that these things do not go away with a quick fix. What happens is you create more problems for yourself than you had before, just more things you will need deliverance from, and this is the plan of the enemy (Satan) the expert in deception. This life was not meant to live with chains around your neck and if the enemy is not exposed no one would ever know the truth that will cause them to seek to become free: The Bible says ***"And ye shall know the truth, and the truth shall make you free" John 8:32 KJV***. If you are going through something with a loved one, meaning someone responsible for taking care of you, please realize that they can only give you what they have received.

We need to take a stand and change unhealthy habits and bad practices with the help of God. Too many people continue with behaviors that they did not like when they were being raised. This is a big problem because bitterness sets in and makes us blind to the fact that we are following the same path that we hate. Here we find generational curses where something bad started with one generation and it gets passed on to the next generation. This must be stopped by someone! Who will take a stand? Why not you?

I did and now I believe many generations after me will walk upright because of the stand the Lord helped me to make. I refuse to walk in the same ways that others walked in before me. In my family bloodline, I was able to see generational curses that dated back to 1935, 80 plus years ago of nobody stopping the cycle of abuse. I am sure that wasn't the first start-out date of the abuse cycle. From my sources that is all that has been told to me at this time.

I find that we as a people put up with things for far too long and then begin to suffer for things and reasons, we shouldn't have ever let enter our lives. I understand how it feels to feel hopeless, this starts something in you, and it is called fear, depression, and many other things. I know that a person can be depressed and not even know it. If you are bursting into tears and need something to take the edge off there is a big problem, there. Early on in my life, I had moments when I would feel sad and would randomly cry, I believe that it was deeply rooted in my life because of rejection and abandonment. Sometimes we allow ourselves to be deceived by self-denial, we clearly see we have a problem but hate to admit it or even face it.

My problem started early on in my childhood. I was abused by my mother; she inflicted a great amount of pain in my life. I never dealt with this pain and my father was not in my life, so it was countless times I felt I was all alone, but God was with me all the time. The history of violence didn't just start with me it was already around before it happened to me. I remember things from the past that made me ask, why me Lord? at the time I couldn't have possibly understood that most of the things I had to walk through would be for God's ministry working/birthing on the inside of me.

I tried to spend most of my time finding out who I was because nobody gave me my identity. After being abused, mistreated, talked about, and trodden down it caused me to have low self-esteem that was accompanied by the spirit of rejection. I didn't even know I had these kinds of problems. I was raised in fear, not love. I was afraid of my mother, and I couldn't talk to her about anything. She put me down and treated me less than a dog.

It is a wonderful blessing that there's no hate in my heart for her, but God .... calmly think about that (BUT GOD). I was born with a hole in my heart and would stop breathing at times (BUT GOD) healed me at 4 months old. I genuinely believe that He put something special in my heart to make it through the life I had to endure. I could not understand why I was made to suffer so much pain, however, I hope all the painful things I have been through will bless the lives of many. I would have to then think that it was all worth it.

No one can change the past and no one can change GOD's plans for your life. I belong to God, and I am thankful for it. There were many things I wasn't taught that could have prevented my mistakes. Everything about my life at that time was a struggle, nothing came to me easy. The Lord knows how to keep us even from death, I felt like I was dying at times. I know God has kept me from so many dangers, from certain kinds of people and bad situations that wanted to swallow me up.

My pain and tears sometimes carried me to sleep. Anger built up inside of me and came out sometimes. I remember I had to be about 5 or 6 years old when I got so mad that I completely tore up a small wooden rocking chair with my bare hands. I was too young to diagnose myself, I could not understand that my abuse was causing me to develop an anger problem. Anger was not just there; I believe that it has become deeply rooted due to the physical abuse I had been experiencing from my mother. When you are a child, you don't always make the best decisions which can lead to discipline, but there is a significant difference between discipline and abuse. I remember being whipped with extension cords that would leave large whelps that made cuts in my skin with bleeding. Why did no one come and save me? I was just a kid and never told anyone what I was going through. There was no one to rescue me and I was too scared to ask for help. I was the only child of my mother for 13 years. Not only was my father absent in my life and I was going through with my mother but the kids at school picked on me as well.

I understand now that the enemy of my soul knew who I would become in the Kingdom of God, and he tried whatever he could to stop me from finding out who God preordained me to be. No things or stumbling blocks he placed before me could stop that which God from the beginning had placed down on the inside of me through His Son Jesus Christ my Lord and Savior. All the hindrances I have experienced God made them work for my good and they are being used to author this book. Some things I was subjected to because of my actions, however a lot of things I had no control over. Most people are walking miracles, I know God stopped death from having me at an early age.

The devil tried to end my life at 16 years

old, I was pregnant and got attacked by my mother. I understand that this was a stressful dilemma to have a pregnant teenager. One night my mom woke me up from my sleep to have me sleep on the couch to let her in after her night out in the town. She returned in the wee hours of the morning, and I let her in the house, and I went upstairs back to bed. At this time, I did not have my own bed in my room, so I laid down in my little brother's bunk beds to go back to sleep. My mom went into the kitchen and was upset when she saw that I had not washed the dishes.

Let me remind you that before her leaving the house I was already sleeping, so why would I be up cleaning if I just went right back to sleep after I locked the door behind her? She called my name and asked where I was, and I told her I was in bed. My mother told me to get out of my brother's bed, so I did, I went into my room and laid down on some garbage bags full of clothes in my closet. The next thing I knew my mom came up the stairs and demanded that I came out of the closet.

I was so scared, so I tried to stay in there because I did not want her to hurt me, (please remember I am 3 months pregnant) she grabbed me out of the closet and sat on my head while punching and digging up my stomach with her nails. I remember being suffocated to the point that I felt like I was taking my last breath with over 200 pounds sitting on top of my head (BUT GOD) Almighty stepped in and pulled all the weight off me. It was like the wind knocked her off me. I believe that God sent an Angel to protect me.

There I was so afraid and in a corner of my room with no place to run, with her standing in front of me. I saw her as if she snapped and then she kicked me upside my head with some Jodeci boots on. I jumped up and took off running down the stairs, I could not get the door opened fast enough and she made it down the stairs where I was. She said, “oh you want to get out Bitc* I will help you”. My mother unlocked the door and grabbed me by my hair and threw me on the porch with a t-shirt, boxers on, and no socks and shoes in the wintertime.

I took off running as fast as I could for 3 blocks without stopping until I made it to my grandparents' house. None of my family knew that I was pregnant, so when I arrived it was 4 in the morning, and I was so shocked that I could not even speak without stuttering. I told my granddad to call the police, he calmed me down and told me to get cleaned up, so I did. After my mom woke up, she had someone to bring her over to my grandparents' house to pick me up. It was then that I told my grandmother that I was pregnant, and my mother was beating on me, “please do not make me go with her”. My grandmother saved me and my unborn son's life, she told my mother to get away from over here and let her know that she would call the police and she did.

The police arrived took reports and photos of my face. Child protective services were contacted, and I was removed from my mother’s house right away. Now here lies the problem, who wants to take in a pregnant teenager. I was taken to a place for troubled teens called Interlink where I remained for two weeks while my family decided who would take care of me. My mother had lost custody of me, and while I was going through a massive investigation with the CPS workers, I saw the pictures the police officer had taken of me after I was attacked. I had no idea how bad I looked; my face was completely swollen and black and blue.

My auntie decided to let me come and stay with her. I was 16 years old and pregnant, they ruled to emancipate me, and the judge had ordered me to have no contact with my mother. For months, I wouldn't talk to anyone, not even my aunt. I was so traumatized. I was in a brand-new city and knew no one, I was so embarrassed that I chose to attend an alternative high school, hoping that I would fit in more there, and I did.

THANK YOU, LORD, FOR SAVING MY LIFE. Can it possibly be a place where people go when they snap, and they don't know what they are doing to you? This kind of rage happens all around the world, somebody gets into a fit of rage and does something they cannot take back. I have seen myself do the unthinkable things in my mind to a person I loved the most in the moment of them hurting me. I thank God that those thoughts never made it into action, this is what we call **malice** meaning (desires to inflict injury, harm, or suffering on another, either because of a hostile impulse or out of deep-seated meanness).

<u>How do you walk through abuse and setbacks without developing anger that over time transforms into rage?</u> the simple answer is FORGIVENESS and

trusting in the LORD to help you. I thought all these years I was walking in forgiveness, but I had been putting it out of my mind, and all this time it was causing me unspeakable anger that I never received healing from. We must face our problems before we can profoundly move on from them. Just overlooking things will not solve any problems.

I believe the first step to getting help is admitting you need help. Sometimes pride, embarrassment, and shame gets in the way of our healing process and causes us to become stagnant, stuck, and bound. You're only powerless by choice, the truth is the enemy tricks you into thinking you are powerless over what you are facing. We must understand there is power for everyone through Christ Jesus, the Word says ***"I***

can do all things through Christ which strenghteneth me" Philippians 4:13 KJV. There were many days I was unable to use this because this scripture was not a known thing to me.

The Bible is the key to which things can be changed. God's word gets on the inside of you and then begins to change & transform your mind and life. This is a process that does not happen overnight but if you continue therein you will begin to see the fruit of God show up in your life. I am a witness and a manifestation of what God's word can do.

Grabbing Bondage by The Throat

Walking out our Freedom

Chapter 2
Letting Go of The Past.

Sometimes it is hard to let go of the past when it's right in front of you. One word or one action can arise and cause you to remember or relive the things you are trying to let go of. How do you keep walking when it is clear that the Lord is doing a work in you, but you can still see some of the old things that had you bound still present in the life of your loved ones that may have been used to hurt you? Wow, this is a great question and I believe the answer is through **patience** meaning (the ability to bear a trial without grumbling). That's right I said a trial because until it is not a now factor in which it affects you then it is still a trial.

When you can walk through something without murmuring and complaining then you can receive your breakthrough. This is a mouth full I know some of you are thinking, what did she say? What is she talking about? Let me explain a little more. In the Bible God leads Israel free from bondage out of Egypt, Moses leads the people into the wilderness, and it was only supposed to be an 11-day trip, but they were in the wilderness for 40 years because of murmuring and complaining. This translates as unbelief. They did not believe the Lord and because of that, they were not able to enter the promised land.

I know it is hard looking at ourselves as a reason our breakthrough isn't coming but the sad thing is we stand in our way all the time. It's time to take another stand and this one will help you move out of your own way to be able to get your blessings. We must make up our mind not to be a blessing blocker in our own life. You cannot move forward with one foot stuck behind you & one in front of you because you won't be able to move. When we are double minded it will cause us to be hindered. Letting go of the past sounds easy but it can be a challenge due to everything you experience that seems to become a part of you, it was never there to be a permanent part of you. These things are just used to build your character, mold you and most of what you're going through is for a greater cause and it's purposed for ministry to help God's hurting people.

Here we find future ministry. The word

past means (previously transpired) from the Greek word (**proginomai #4266**), so it should be easy to let go of the past things that have previously happened in your life, however some of these things we need to be healed & delivered from. The Bible tells us ***"Wherefore seeing we also are compassed about with a great cloud of witnesses, let us lay aside every weight, and the sin which doths so easily beset us, and let us run with patience the race that is set before us," Hebrews 12:1 KJV***. These issues that we carry around with us have become weights that will weigh us down and make us unable to operate properly. This causes us to relive the sins of our past which besets us, meaning your past is on all sides harassing & surrounding you to take you under. To be weight free you must let go of the past.

I know you will remember everything from your past, but you don't have to be taunted or be judged by no man with it. The Bible tells us in the last part of ***Hebrews 12:1*** ***"<u>:and let us run with patience the race that is set before us,</u>"*** now we see that word **patience** again which we talked about at the beginning of this chapter which means (The ability to bare a trial without grumbling) this verse tells us how to run the race. Life is the race you are running and <u>who is willing to let go of the past?</u> (I AM) now it is time to run the life race.

- ✓ **<u>3 Key points for letting go of the past.</u>**

- ✓ **<u>Point #1</u> {Through *<u>patience</u>*} (The ability to bear trial without grumbling.) *Romans 5:3-5 "And***

not only so, we glory in tribulation also: knowing that tribulation worketh patience; and patience, experience; and experience, hope and hope maketh not ashamed;

If you give praise & thanks to God while you are in a state or time of great affliction it will produce the ability to bare trials without complaining. You will accumulate understanding and be able to rely on God's blessings, and provisions and expect future good from Him. After all of this you will not be made ashamed because God is faithful, patience brings breakthroughs so you can be an operating system that can receive promises and blessings from God.

- ✓ **Point #2 {Getting out of your**

way}

You cannot move forward by being stuck in the past because you will stay bound and potentially kill your chances of living life.

Genesis 19:26 "But his wife looked back from behind him, and she became a pillar of salt" KJV

Here we see an example of someone standing in their way and in this case, Lot's wife was caught up in the past sin that God was delivering her family out of. You cannot be consumed with your past because it can be used to destroy your life and your hope for the manifestation of your future.

- ✓ **Point # 3 {Laying aside every weight}**

The word weight from the Greek word (Ogkos#3591) means (burden)- **[hindrance].** ***I know that the past can be a burden & hindrance that can stop you from moving forward if you don't lay it down. The Word of God tells us to lay them aside, Hebrews 12:1.*** *Who can run a life race with weights on them?* ***You might be able to get along for a little while, however after some time has passed your soul will be run down to the point that you won't be able to finish your life race and journey you are trying to complete. It's easier to run weight-free, so let go of the past to be freely used by God.***

Chapter 3
We Must Walk in Forgiveness.

Sometimes walking in forgiveness seems to be so hard. I have learned that when you're wounded it makes it very difficult to do when you haven't received your healing. I never knew that unforgiveness had become my behavior and characteristics that I walked in. Let's take a moment to talk about unforgiveness. Unforgiveness has so many dangers that I am very sure that people don't even realize how serious the effects are. We open the doors to demons. Our fellowship with God becomes hindered, please see ***Mark 11:22-26***.

I never knew that my anger issues were attached to walking in unforgiveness. I had outbursts of anger, and it was waiting underneath the surface to explode. I thought that everyone needed to understand my pain because I was unhealed. If I am honest it does seem to bring a little comfort to know that others understand your dilemma, but it is truly not necessary. All this time I thought that because I still showed myself present in the life of my mom I was walking in forgiveness.

I was putting band-aids on my wounds and not dealing with my past pain. To be transparent I wished that I would have had a conversation with my mother and simply asked her why she treated me the way she treated me. I loved her so much and most of my biggest problems were that I never really wanted to hurt her by addressing our issues, even though I was hurting. We suffer and

never confront the source of our sufferings. I think that this causes an empty hole in our lives.
I really wanted to have a healthy relationship with my mom, and I also felt that I needed it for my development. I never understood what it could be like, to have mother-daughter dates, intimate conversations, and a safe place to be me. I never had the chance to enjoy my mom. I always had up a guard because I needed to protect myself, so I thought. Our relationship was toxic and unhealthy.

Missed opportunities are sometimes ones that you can never get back. I remember having a conversation with my father about my relationship with my mother and he told me right then to confront her and talk about it. I had started writing my first book and it was just about the abuse that I endured in my childhood and so I told my dad about it, and he urged me to talk to her and I never did. I packed away the writings and never completed the book at all. I don't understand why I did not talk to her, because it could have brought both of us so much-needed freedom.

One of the worst feelings you can ever have is missed chances to make things right. I waited too long to give her a chance to explain what she was facing that led her to the abusive patterns I was experiencing. In my mind I treated her with the utmost respect, however, I had triggers that kept me distant. I truly wanted to make amends, but it was very difficult because the abuse was still there, it was tailored differently since I became an adult. There is a big difference between childhood abuse and abuse in adulthood, neither one is favorable. As a child, I had no choice but the circumstances were much different as an adult.

I started confronting all the things that I spent years carrying, without my mother, it was just between me and God. I denounced every stronghold that I faced from abuse and I began to let it go. I think that when we suffer, we take ownership of being treated poorly that does not belong to us, and we cannot even see that it has made us bound, and created limitations that stops us from gaining our breakthrough.

I had to make peace with my upbringing, and I had to forgive my mother even without an apology. I remember one time many years ago when I did try to talk to my mother about the attack when

I was 16 and she never admitted to kicking me upside the head, from that time I lost hope of any kind of reconciliation of our past differences. There was evidence that I needed things to change so I started doing self-deliverance. The first thing I did was renounce all the weights that I had been carrying.

I told God that the abuse I suffered was not my stuff and I broke all agreements with any generational curses that had been plaguing my bloodline in the name of Jesus. We must understand our mouth holds power and because we have authority and power that has been given to us by God. I started decreeing my freedom and it helped me to make peace with my mom. I also rejected her part in my life that caused me pain. I began to understand that she was not able to provide me with something that she did not possess.

In the moment of my breakthrough as I prayed, I remember feeling like I had to vomit and coughing up what seem to be a thick mucus. Here I was for the first time of my life getting free from my past bondage. I decided that I wanted to move on and advance in my life and have my new beginning. I felt so much lighter. I did not realize that I was being setup for the next chapter of my life.

Now I was able to confess that I was no longer walking in unforgiveness, and my freedom came from God. We must come to the end of ourselves and partner with God, we must surrender to God and then we can obtain our freedom. We must do away with pride, it will keep us bound. Sometimes we think of ourselves as weak if we let go of our past hurts. We even think that our oppressor is getting away with the offenses, so we keep them locked up in a prison in our heart to our own disadvantage. Those people are free to live their lives and we are the ones stuck.

God is so powerful and all knowing, I had no idea that maybe 1 or 2 months later that my mother was going to die. I was free and able to properly put her to rest. When I received the call from the hospital at 1:23 am on 12/5/22, the doctor told me that my mom was pronounced deceased, it was a very surreal moment. I didn't realize it in the moment, but God had provided me a way out of unforgiveness to walk strong and complete everything that was needed in serving my mother for the last time.

I just want to let you all into a transparent moment, I walked into the hospital to claim my mom's body and to see her there all alone broke my heart, I felt so much sorrow. Remember earlier in this chapter how I stated that unforgiveness kept me distant, and I saw her and felt SO GUILTY for not being there. For days I could not get that image of her there all alone out of my head. Honestly some of her being alone was part her fault, she was very stubborn and refused to communicate with me, it kept me out of the loop. I could have put forth more of an effort to press into her space, but broken people will put up walls to prevent more hurt from happening.

Some people have a chance to fix

things and others live in regret. I hope my story will give you the tools to make healthy choices to help you walk out your freedom. If I had the opportunity, I would have done things differently, I would not let my pride drive me away from my mom and I would have sown more seeds towards us having a chance at a healthy relationship. Both of my parents are now resting in heaven, and I never would have thought that I would be so young without my parents. My sorrow comes when I think about having no parents.

I never realized my desperation of not ever being like my mother was a driving force that pushed me to greatness in motherhood, relationships, and many other things. My mom played a very important role in helping me become me, the sad thing is, I never told her that because I never saw it from this perspective until now. When you are healed you can see clearly. It is imperative that we walk in forgiveness to be forgiven by God. No bondage is worth losing our right to forgiveness. We have been called for this time to walk bold and free. Don't ever go backward!

Grabbing Bondage by The Throat

Walking out our Freedom

Chapter 4
Knowing The Power Within & Who You Are.

This is a time for all born-again believers to understand the power that God has placed on the inside of you. First, let me say to those of you who have not yet accepted Jesus Christ as your Lord & Savior let's take this time to ask the Lord to come into your heart. ***Romans 10:9 "That if thou shalt confess with thy mouth the Lord Jesus, and shalt believe in thine heart that God hath raised him from the dead, thou shalt be saved" KJV***. When you pray just confess that Jesus is Lord and ask Him to come into your heart, also believe God raised him from the dead and you are now saved, I welcome all of you into the family of God, God bless you, and congratulations.

We have the **kingdom of God** within us, this means (God's kingly rule; Wherever God rules) the Word says ***"For the kingdom of God is not in word, but in power "1 Corinthians 4:20 KJV***. God's kingly rule is within, and it is powerful. The Holy Spirit is within you, you have the power that comes from Heaven inside of you, God has given us all things because He has given everything to Jesus and God said WE ARE joint heirs with Christ Jesus. God has placed all power in Christ's hands. Jesus said all the works that He did, greater works will WE do.

You have the power and authority given by Christ to tread on scorpions, see

Luke 10:19 & Luke 9:1. You have the power to speak things into existence through the power of the tongue, God created us in His image, to sum it up WE HAVE the attributes of God within us. We are vessels used by God to establish His will here, on the earth. Look at yourself the way God does, you are the apple of His eye, a peculiar people, more than a conqueror, the righteousness of Christ Jesus, the head and not the tail, above and not beneath. You are greatly loved by God and knowing this activates POWER & FAITH of God in your life. YOU ARE NOT POWERLESS.

You Are.

- ***You Are! A new creature in Christ. 2Corinthians 5:17***
- ***You Are! The temple of the Holy***

Spirit. 1Corinthians 6:19

- ***<u>You Are!</u> Delivered from the power of darkness and translated in God's kingdom. Colossians 1:13***
- ***<u>You Are!</u> Redeemed from the curse of the law of sin and death. 1Peter 1:18,19 & Galatians 3:13***
- ***<u>You Are!</u> Blessed. Deuteronomy 28:1-12 & Galatians 3:9***
- ***<u>You Are!</u> Holy and without blame before Him in love. 1Peter 1:6 & Ephesians 1:4***
- ***<u>You Are!</u> The Elect of God. Colossians 3:12 & Romans 8:33***
- ***<u>You Are!</u> Established to the end. Romans 1:11***
- ***<u>You Are!</u> Set free. John 8:31-33***
- ***<u>You Are!</u> Strong in the Lord. Ephesians 6:10***
- ***<u>You Are!</u> Dead to sin. Romans 6:1,11 & 1 Peter 2:24***
- ***<u>You Are!</u> More than a conqueror. Romans 8:37***

- ***You Are!* Joint heirs with Christ. Romans 8:13**
- ***You Are!* Sealed with the Holy Spirit of promise, Ephesians 1:13**
- ***You Are!* In Christ by His doing. 1 Corinthians 1:30**
- ***You Are!* Accepted in the beloved. Ephesians 1:16**
- ***You Are!* Complete in Him. Colossians 2:10**
- ***You Are!* Crucified with Christ. Galatians 2:20**
- ***You Are!* Alive with Christ. Galatians 2:20**
- ***You Are!* Free from condemnation. John 5:24**
- ***You Are!* Reconciled to God. 2 Corinthians 5:18**
- ***You Are!* Qualified to share in His inheritance. Colossians 1:12**
- ***You Are!* Firmly rooted built up, established in your faith and overflowing with thanksgiving.**

Colossians 2:7

- ***<u>You Are!</u> Born of God and the evil cannot touch you. 1John 5:18***
- ***<u>You Are!</u> Overtaken with blessing. Deuteronomy 28:2***
- ***<u>You Are!</u> The light of the world. Matthew 5:14***
- ***<u>You Are!</u> The salt of the earth. Matthew 5:13***
- ***<u>You Are!</u> The apple of your Father's eye. Deuteronomy 32:10***
- ***<u>You Are!</u> Healed by the stripes of Jesus. 1Peter 2:25 & Isaiah 53:6***
- ***<u>You Are!</u> A child of God. John 1:12 & Romans 8:16***
- ***<u>You Are!</u> Christ's friend. John 15:15***
- ***<u>You Are!</u> One with Christ. Galatians 3:26,28***
- ***<u>You Are!</u> A citizen of Heaven and seated in Heaven right now. Philippians 3:20 & Ephesians 2:6***
- ***<u>You Are!</u> The enemy of the devil.***

1Peter 5:8

- ***You Are! Established, anointed, and sealed by God in Christ. 2 Corinthians 1:21***

Most people don't understand that the power of God becomes available as soon as we become believers and followers of Christ. Once you take the first steps to receive salvation it is time to go to the feet of Jesus and start building an intimate relationship with God, this comes through spending time reading the bible and praying to God. We must be dependent upon God for everything. This will be a process so please give yourself time and let God take you on your journey to newness.

Confess these **YOU ARE's,** over your life every day so you can speak about yourself the way God does. By doing so you will unlock the power within **YOU** and come to know **WHO YOU ARE** in Christ. When you learn who God says YOU ARE then you have become **UNSTOPPABLE** to the enemies of this world. If God be for you, who can be against you? **NO ONE.**

Chapter 5
Walking Unashamed.

In the previous chapter, we talked about the power within us and who God says we are. So now let's talk about how to walk. Now with everything you know it's time to move on with the life God planned for you to live. The first and most important thing is **not putting any man on the throne of your heart.** This is a form of idol worship and a blessing blocker that makes God angry.

You can't make the mistake of lifting someone higher than God, this very thing will cause us to depart from God. There is no way to walk with two Gods, you will love one and hate the other, and you can't serve God and mammon, see ***Matthew 6:24***. We have been called to walk in freedom and not bondage or fear. It is time to walk in the light of the Father. Don't allow yourself to walk in your past, you are intended to learn from it and pass along your testimony to those of God's choosing.

Walking for Christ is how we experience real freedom for ourselves. No one can see all the chains on them without the Father's help & without reading the Bible. It is great to hear a word from somebody else but at the end of the day, you need to know the word for yourself. How can you know when the enemy is speaking a lie to you? You can't if you don't know God's word.

Walking with God is an honor, a privilege, and a responsibility. We are not called unto ourselves but unto God. How can you not possibly give Him everything you have? (Calmly think about that). God wants our whole heart not part of it or half of it but our **WHOLE HEART**. I have seen God's hand work and move in my life, and I know God is worth dying to self.

He is better than a friend, He knows all and is concerned for you more than anybody could ever be. The walk of a believer is the Christian life which is a life that is all about living for the Lord His way according to the word of God. The word **walk** is defined as, (One's conduct of life) this meaning is only measured by God's way and His word, not by human meaning. This walk has a lot to do with how you speak & think.

You cannot walk victoriously without

walking and talking like God does. We need to have a renewed mind. The Bible tells us that the word is our source to gaining the transformation of our mind and heart, the word of God washes us and cleanses us and proves the will of God, please see ***Romans 12:2***. We must be willing to die to self for us to become the polished product that God can get glory from. Most often we are so comfortable being in control of us that we don't submit to our Heavenly Father, and it prevents us from gaining the total breakthrough that God has for us.

God said He has set before you life & death, blessings & curses, it is your choice of how you want to live and walk. God is not going to make you do anything, but He will continue to show you the right way, it's up to you to follow Him. If you have been changed &

affected in any way by God. Why would you want to go back to rotten living? (Food for thought). God is faithful and can perform everything He said he would. All His promises will come to pass. Are you willing to endure to the end? I HOPE SO, because I AM.

Sometimes God shows us things so we can have hope to continue, we must understand that what he shows us comes with a process, He must get us completely ready for it, so don't lose hope. Give praise and thanksgiving to God while you're in a state and time of great affliction because it will produce the ability to bear trials without complaining (simply put, we will gain patience). You will accumulate understanding that will empower you to rely on God's blessings, and provisions and expect future good from Him, see

Romans 5:3-5. Walking with God is a lifetime job, you don't do it one day and the next day stop, this is a continual process for your life to bring God the glory.

When you think about walking through your life remember it is not about you but the will of God for your life. The moment that you become saved, your job is to get to know God and find out who He called you to be and what He has called you to do. I once heard a Man of God say "We are life stealers" …. WOW, I never thought about being a stealer of life, but there is truth in this matter, every day we don't yield to the calling of God we ARE stealing LIFE. God made us for a reason, and we should become just what He made us for. God has given us the power of decision; however, He lives on the inside of us and wants to direct our path.

He waits for us to come to Him to be shown the way, don't be your guide because God will never steer you the wrong way. When you are in line with God you can walk in total peace and freedom. We cannot be people pleasers and walk with the Lord. We cannot be **friends** with the world meaning we can't be in love with, trust, or highly esteem the world because we will become enemies with God. The world does not operate in the things of God. When you walk with the Lord your mind must be renewed, the old way of life is useless in the kingdom of God.

Take a deep breath because walking with God is not impossible it just takes time; God will help you. The more you study & learn the word the more equipped you will become. The Bible has an answer to every question you will possibly have. God will bring you through! Your job is making the choice not to stop walking on your journey. There are going to be many things you don't understand, just have faith that God has everything under control.

Faith is the key to your success in your Godly walk. The Bible says ***"For as the body without the spirit is dead, so faith without works is dead also" James 2:26 KJV***, there must be continual work done for God whom you put your hope in. The word says ***"Now faith is the substance of things hoped for, the evidence of things not seen" Hebrews 11:1 KJV***, faith is having confidence without proof. You cannot walk with God without having faith, it is impossible to please God without it, see ***Hebrews 11:6***. Keep walking because God promised you won't be ashamed.

Walking out our Freedom

Chapter 6
Victory in The Battle.

Know that the battle belongs to the Lord, and he wins every battle. A battle is an armed combat between two enemy forces, it's also being engaged in warfare and to fight and or make war. Every battle you encounter remember that it is already won. I know you can lose focus and not think about how Jesus has already won the battle and sometimes want to take the fight into your own hands, but this is not the way. Our true fight is not against flesh and blood but against **principalities** and **powers**, against **rulers of darkness of this world** and against **spiritual wickedness in high places**. **See *Ephesians 6:12*.**

<u>*Making Plain the enemy*</u>

→ **<u>Principalities</u> – a powerful ruler, or the rule of someone in authority, demonic spirits and demons. They are the chief rulers and have the highest rank in Satan's kingdom.**

→ **<u>Powers</u> – oppressors, in great power, strong, terrible, and violent. Authorities derive their power from and execute the will of the chief rulers.**

→ **<u>Rulers of the darkness</u> – spiritual world rulers.**

→ **<u>Spiritual wickedness</u> – wicked spirits of Satan in the heavens.**

The attributes of Satan

- **The Father of Lies**– see John 8:44

Father- is a male parent, one who raises children. Lies- are when one intentionally tells an untruth. Satan raises his children to intentionally speak nontruths.

- **Deceiver** – see Revelations 12:9

Deceiver- is one that deludes or misleads.
He imposes a misleading belief upon someone by causing them to have the wrong idea or impression about someone or something.

- **Adversary** – see 1 Peter 5:8

Adversary- is one who actively opposes.

Known as the devil and the chief opponent of God.
Chief – pertaining to the highest rank or office.
In other words, he is the highest-ranked opponent in opposition to God and His people.

We are told to be sober meaning to be marked by moderation, temperance, and seriousness. We are to be vigilant meaning we are to be alert and watchful.

Satan's camp is highly organized, and his kingdom is not divided against itself.

We see the structure.

I. Principalities
II. Powers
III. Rulers of darkness of this world

IV. Spiritual wickedness in high places

These are the governments of Satan.

- Above are the recognized ruler ships.

→ The **principalities** are rulers and governments made up of angels and demons. The fallen angels of heaven are with Satan, and they are supernatural opponents.

→ The **powers** have authority, control and influence in the supernatural realm.

→ The **rulers of darkness** of this world are the ones who govern or exercise authority where there is no light, there is ignorance with moral and spiritual destitution in this temporal place we live.

→ **Spiritual wickedness** in high places is the unseen realm of all forms of evil in positions of power and authority.

The kingdom of darkness has different levels of rankings and is extremely organized.
The bible says that Satan can't cast out Satan. If he is divided against himself then how shall his kingdom stand? Matthew 12:26. The strategy of the enemy is to work together with the official officers of the kingdom of darkness to complete their commanded assignment which is to steal, kill and destroy, see John 10:10.

Now that we have made the enemy

plain let's talk about how to execute a plan to destroy the strategies of the enemy.

Destroying Satan's Strategies

1. **Submit yourself unto God - see James 4:7**

- When we submit ourselves, we are yielding to Gods governance and His authority. This pushes us to the things of God like praying, praising and reading the bible. When we are so dialed in to the heavenly things and resist the devil, the bible says that he will run away from us, God's presence has made us become dangerous to the enemy.

2. **Put on the whole armor of God**

– see Ephesians 6:11,13-18

- Armor is metal coverings formerly worn by soldiers or warriors to protect the body in battle. We are in battle, and we are soldiers in the army of the Lord, so we need the armor that God gave us to protect us because we are His Body which needs protection.

→ Our Armor Consists of

1. **The Truth** (The word of God/Jesus)
2. **Righteousness** (Given to us by God through Jesus Christ – Breastplate)
3. **Gospel of Peace** (Feet that walk in the way of the peace of the

Lord)

4. **Faith** (Protects us from the fury darts of the enemy by keeping us covered – shield)

5. **Salvation** (Making Christ the head of your life, our head protection – helmet)

6. **The Spirit** (Our ultimate weapon that's wrapped with the Word of God, Jesus Christ – Our sword)

7. **Praying** (We pray to God through His Spirit and expect His answers through the manifestation or our request.

We must remember that we have the power and all the tools that have been given to us that makes us mighty.

Grabbing Bondage by The Throat

Walking out our Freedom

Chapter 7
Never Go Back to Bondage.

We have been fully equipped and cannot afford to go back into bondage. Now that we have confronted the roots of our issues, we need to shift our focus to being filled with spiritual furniture. The Bible tells us that after the demons/unclean spirits are evicted from our houses he goes to and from to find new residences. Please read ***Matthew 12:43-45.*** Let's break this down some.

When we are in bondage of any kind, and we go through a deliverance process we through God can maintain our freedom. Whenever there is any form of uncleanness and we have been cleansed, the enemy will find no other place to rest and will want to return back to set up shop inside of us but he has new friends(demons) the bible states that he has 7 more spirits that are more powerful than itself.

If we thought the condition that we were in previously was bad, this situation would present as the worst. I never remember anyone instructing me on what to do after I had gained my freedom. The word talks about the house being found empty and swept cleanly decorated. The house that the scriptures are speaking about is referring to us. The Bible sometimes speaks in parables.

We must fill our houses with spiritual food. Once we are delivered it is now time to be filled with God's word, prayer, and relationship with God. I never want to be bound again and I hope that you do not want to be either. When something is put out it must be replaced. Let's take a small detour. When God woke me up and brought me into a relationship with Him, I was walking in a large number of things of the world.

I used to hang out, rap for the world, and many other things. As I started reading the Bible all my normal activities became questionable. My house was being processed to be cleaned and as I started reading the bible my normal started to not make sense to me. There was a conflict of interest. I was going through my deliverance process and becoming aware of the truth through the word of God because it was changing me. I noticed that all the things that I once enjoyed had become things that I no longer wanted to do.

I remember taking all the lyrics that I wrote that were secular and throwing them away without any new music. In this case I would have to say that my house was cleansed, but because I continued to read the Bible my house was no longer empty, it was being filled by the living word of God. There was no longer a place for the enemy to come back to, then God started giving me lyrics that brought Him glory.

The moral of what we are discussing is replacing your unhealthy habits, and practices with things that are of the Kingdom of GOD. We have been given the power to decide to maintain our freedom. I believe that it is always in our best interest to follow in the path of righteousness, it sometimes seems very difficult to practice those things that are right. It is very important for us to keep showing up for us.

We must realize that in order to continuing moving forward we have to simply forgive ourselves and others who played a part in our hurt. Please remember this is no longer your stuff and you no longer live at this address. Self-reflection is very necessary; we have to remember to encourage ourselves to continue in a positive state. Do not allow others to drag you back to your past because you have been made free.

We are now new creations, and we have a new opportunity to build better and stronger. It is so important to cut off relationships that are unhealthy and don't serve a purpose in God's journey for your life, bottom line everyone won't make this new transition with you but let God lead you while making different decisions, He will make it plain. I am very proud of us; God has put the ball in our court, it's time to be great and stay free.

Chapter 8
Power Prayer & Closing

Lord, I pray that you empower us to war in your SPIRIT to shut down every door and every portal of the enemy, that he be annihilated by the fire of the Holy Ghost. We renounce every generational curse cycle in the name of Jesus. We close every demonic portal and gate in the name of Jesus. Every prince demon we command you out by the authority given from heaven through God's dear son Jesus Christ. We cause calamity on the father of lies Satan and his army of principalities and powers, rulers of the darkness of this world, spiritual wickedness in high places along with every ancestral demon in the name of Jesus. We annihilate every generational word curse attached to our bloodline we return every work of the enemy back to its original sender in the name of Jesus. We break down every wall that was placed up by the devil Satan, we shatter every work from every witch, warlock, enchanting demon, every sorcerer, and enchantments in the name of Jesus. We muzzle the mouth of the soothsayer from the kingdom of darkness. We choke the life out of every evil trap, plot, and snare. We release the protection of God into the life of the believer in the name of Jesus. We close every door sent from Satan. We grab every bit of bondage by the throat and bring it into captivity in the name of Jesus Christ. We move every mountain of lack, debt, impoverishment, stoppages, blocks, hindrances, failures, and setbacks. We decree things to be changed for the betterment of the Body of Christ and for the good of the believer in the name of Jesus. We release the newness of life and replace all that was lost/stolen in double in the name of Jesus. Lord, we ask that you fill our house so that the enemy can't return and that he be forever banished from generation to generation from this day on. We speak in the name of Jesus Christ our Lord the Son of God. We come against any recoil and retaliation from the enemy in the name of Jesus. Lord, we thank you for answering this prayer HALLEUJAH we pray in Jesus's name amen.

Grabbing Bondage by The Throat

Walking out our Freedom

Closing

Please use this book as a reference to maintain the freedom that God provided us through our precious Lord Jesus Christ. Please remain in good spirits and continue to fight the good fight of faith, you have all of heaven cheering you on. We must remember that we need each other, we are the body of Christ, and every part of the body is very intricate and necessary. Let's connect with like-minded believers, become iron that sharpens iron, and push the Kingdom agenda of Heaven here on earth.

God bless you and keep you until we meet again.

Shawneesha Cooper is a multi-talented individual from Saginaw, Michigan. She is a pastor, rap artist, author, educator, and entrepreneur who is committed to fulfilling her life's purpose. She has a strong faith in God and uses her journey to inspire and empower others.

To book Pastor Cooper please visit her website: www.outpourglobal.com

www.ingramcontent.com/pod-product-compliance
Lightning Source LLC
LaVergne TN
LVHW020654100826
845148LV00012B/2489

* 9 7 9 8 2 1 8 4 3 1 3 6 5 *